The Secret Agent

JOSEPH CONRAD

Serie

Pearson Education Limited
Edinburgh Gate, Harlow,
Essex CM20 2JE, England
and Associated Companies throughout the world.

ISBN 0 582 41769 4

First published 1907
Published by Penguin Books by arrangement with the trustees of the
Joseph Conrad Estate and J. M. Dent & Sons Ltd 1963
This adaptation first published by Penguin Books 1998
Published by Addison Wesley Longman Limited and Penguin Books Ltd. 1998
New edition first published 1999

5 7 9 10 8 6 4

Typeset by Digital Type, London
Set in 11/14pt Bembo
Printed in Spain by Mateu Cromo, S. A. Pinto (Madrid)

Published by Pearson Education Limited in association with
Penguin Books Ltd, both companies being subsidiaries of Pearson Plc

For a complete list of the titles available in the Penguin Readers series please write to your local
Pearson Education office or to: Marketing Department, Penguin Longman Publishing,
80 Strand, London, WC2R 0RL

Contents

Introduction

'When I say we want action,' Mr Vladimir went on, 'I don't mean that people have to die. We just want to frighten people. Buildings are enough. But which buildings? That's the question. What do you think, Mr Verloc?'

Mr Verloc didn't know. He said nothing …

Mr Verloc is a fat man who owns a bookshop in London. He is happily married to a pretty young woman called Winnie. Winnie's brother, Stevie, lives with them. Stevie is a good-looking boy but he has a problem. There is something wrong with his head and he can't remember things. So Mr Verloc and Winnie have to look after him.

Mr Verloc is very lazy. He just wants to be comfortable and to look after his shop. But he is also an anarchist. He belongs to a group of anarchists who have meetings in his house. They all want to see a revolution in Britain, but Mr Verloc doesn't really want to do very much about it. He wants a revolution just to happen.

Mr Vladimir works in the Russian Embassy. He orders Mr Verloc to bomb an important scientific building in London. This is very difficult for Mr Verloc. Will he do the job? *Can* he do the job? And what happens when the plan all goes terribly wrong?

The Secret Agent (1907) takes place in London in the late 1880s. At this time in Europe and Russia the political movement called anarchism, which disagreed with all forms of government, was becoming popular. Conrad's story is very exciting, with surprises on every page. But it is far more than just an adventure story. It is also a study of the badness that can lie at the heart of man.

Joseph Conrad was very unusual. He was an adventurer as well as a great writer. He was born Joseph Teodor Konrad Korzeniowski in 1857 in an area of Poland which is now part of the Ukraine. His parents were both Polish and were very interested in politics. They were against the Russians who were strong in this part of Poland, and in the end the family had to leave their home. Both his parents were dead by the time Conrad was eleven years old. He was then looked after by his uncle.

Conrad joined a French ship at the age of seventeen and spent the next twenty years at sea. He sailed around much of the world and had many adventures. A lot of the stories which he wrote later were about the sea. The year 1878 was a very important one in Conrad's life. He tried to kill himself, and later began to work on English ships. In 1886 he became British.

In 1894 Conrad decided to stop being a sailor and spend all his time writing. He married Jessie George in 1895 and they had two sons. In the same year his book, *Almayer's Folly*, came out. This was the first of many books by Conrad which takes place at sea.

Although many important British writers thought Conrad's writing was great, he was not really successful until 1913 with his book *Chance*. Conrad died in 1924, at the age of sixty-seven. By the time of his death, he was both rich and successful as a writer.

Conrad is one of the greatest writers in English literature. He was much more than just a writer of adventure stories, and is seen as one of the most important writers in the 'Modernist' movement. Other writers who belonged to this movement were the Irish writer, James Joyce, and the American poet, T. S. Eliot. These writers understood that the way of life in one country is not better or worse than the way of life in another. Conrad travelled widely and many of his stories are about people's lives in different parts of the world.

Conrad's novels are mainly about the badness in people. People love others and are then hurt by them, or they hurt themselves. In *The Secret Agent*, Winnie loves Verloc, her husband, and is badly hurt by him. Almost none of the people in *The Secret Agent* are good people. The anarchists are either lazy or cold-blooded. The detectives are just interested in money and getting information. Only Winnie and Stevie are good, but at the end of the story Winnie also becomes bad. All the people in the story do things that neither they nor the reader think they will do. Conrad's own family was political and *The Secret Agent* is the world's first political story, with spies, dishonest policemen, bombs and murder. The story shows Conrad's feelings of hatred towards Russians, who took over Poland, his country, and killed his parents.

Conrad wrote many books. The most famous ones *are Lord Jim, Nostromo, Heart of Darkness* and *The Secret Agent*. Many people think that this book is one of the best books that anyone has ever written in the English language. *The Secret Agent* is also a film, with Bob Hoskins, Gerard Depardieu, and Patricia Arquette.

Chapter 1   The Lazy Shopkeeper

Mr Verloc went out in the morning, leaving his wife's brother to look after the shop and his wife to look after her brother. This was all right, because very few customers came into the shop before the evenings.

The shop was small, and so was the house. They lived in a back room behind the shop, and in the bedrooms upstairs. The house was dirty, in a poor part of London. The shop was like a square box. In the daytime the door stayed closed; in the evenings it was open a little.

The shop window showed pictures of dancing-girls without many clothes on. There were also mysterious boxes and packets, some books and some newspapers. The books were not the sort that anyone showed to respectable people. No one seemed interested in the newspapers, which were yellow with age. Mr Verloc's anarchist friends wrote them.

The shop's customers were either very young men, who waited by the window for a time before suddenly going in, or older men with dirty clothes. They pushed their hands into the pockets of their coats and pulled their hats low over their faces before going into the shop. Customers went into the shop quickly, but they could not escape the old bell. As soon as anyone came into the shop, the bell made a loud sound.

At the sound of the bell Mr Verloc left the back room and came into the shop. He was a fat man, with heavy eyes. When you saw him, you thought that he slept in his clothes. In most businesses, people need to wear nice clothes and to look nice. But in Mr Verloc's business it didn't matter. His customers paid the high prices that Mr Verloc asked, without worrying about the clothes of the shopkeeper.

Sometimes Mrs Verloc came into the shop at the sound of the bell.
Winnie Verloc was a young, pretty woman.

Sometimes Mrs Verloc came into the shop at the sound of the bell. Winnie Verloc was a young, pretty woman. When she came into the shop, young customers couldn't meet her eyes. They bought something useless, like a pencil. They paid too much for the pencil, but as soon as they were out of the shop, they threw it away angrily.

Customers were not the only people to push through the dirty door. In the evenings Mr Verloc sometimes had visitors. They said hello to Mrs Verloc and walked past her into the back room.

Mr Verloc was a lazy man who liked his life to be comfortable. And his life *was* comfortable. He had some money. His wife looked after him, and she seemed happy. She seemed to admire him, and what more can a respectable man want?

When Winnie was younger, Winnie's mother had a small hotel. Some men stayed in the hotel for months or years, and others stayed just for a few nights while they had business in London. Winnie helped her mother to look after the hotel. The men all liked her. She was pretty, and she had beautiful, thick black hair. She was also quiet, and didn't talk much, and the men liked that too. Mr Verloc stayed at the hotel when he was in London. He seemed respectable, and he always had money.

When Mr Verloc and Winnie got married, they decided to leave the hotel. Winnie's mother sold it, and Mr Verloc and his new wife took some furniture from it for their new house. And along with the furniture went Stevie. Winnie's mother was glad that she didn't have to worry about Stevie. Mr Verloc had money; Mr Verloc could look after Stevie. And Winnie always loved Stevie.

Stevie was a problem. He was a good-looking boy, but weak. He could read and write, but was not much help in the hotel. There was something wrong with his head. He could not remember things. Outside, he could not find his way home, and could not remember his address. Sudden questions and noises worried him a lot. His sentences were never good, but when he was worried they were worse. He got angry easily, and then he could speak only one or two words.

So Stevie came with the furniture to Mr Verloc's new house, with the shop in front. And there he sat all day, making circles on pieces of paper, while Winnie looked at him from time to time, in the way that a mother looks at her child.

Chapter 2   A Dangerous Plan

Mr Verloc left the house at 10.30 in the morning. It was unusually early for him. The sun shone, and he walked past Hyde Park where men and women were riding horses, and people were walking. He wore his blue coat, his boots were black and shiny, and his face seemed fresh and clean. His heavy eyes were more awake than usual. Carriages drove past on the roads, pulled by horses, with women's faces at the windows.

Mr Verloc could see that the people in the carriages and in the park were rich. The rich were weak and they had to guard themselves and their money against the poor. So the rich were afraid of the poor, and the poor hated the rich. Mr Verloc was an anarchist, and he wanted to see a revolution in Britain. He did not want to *do* very much, because he was lazy, but he wanted a revolution just to happen. So he was happy that the rich and the poor were enemies.

Mr Verloc arrived in Chesham Square and knocked on the door of a large house. It was the Embassy of a foreign country. A servant opened the door and Mr Verloc walked inside. He pulled a letter from his pocket and showed it to the servant, who looked at it and then took Mr Verloc to a room. Mr Verloc waited in the room for a few minutes, and then he heard a door open behind him.

Mr Verloc knocked on the door of a large house.
It was the Embassy of a foreign country.

At first, when he turned, he saw only black clothes, the top of a head, and some papers. The man was reading the papers as he walked into the room. He went over to the table and put the papers down on it. Then he put on some glasses and turned to look at Mr Verloc.

'My name is Vladimir,' the man said, and he picked up the papers again. 'We have here some of your reports.'

Mr Verloc waited. What was this man going to say?

'We're not happy about the police in this country,' Mr Vladimir continued. He seemed tired.

For the first time since he left his home that morning, Mr Verloc opened his lips. 'Every country has its police,' he said. But the Embassy man just continued to look at him, so Mr Verloc went on: 'You know that I cannot do anything about the police here.'

'We want to see something happen,' Mr Vladimir said. 'Something big. You can do that, can't you?'

Mr Verloc didn't answer. 'The police here are too soft,' Mr Vladimir said. He went and sat down behind a desk. 'We want them to be harder. Then ordinary people will be afraid of them ... and then ordinary people will want a change, a revolution perhaps. Do you see? People here do not hate the police enough.'

'Of course,' said Mr Verloc, who was not unintelligent. 'If you read my reports, you will see that the ordinary people of this country are already unhappy. Things are getting quite dangerous here.'

'I have read your reports,' said Mr Vladimir. 'I cannot understand why you wrote them. They are useless. We already *know* things are dangerous. Why do you think we use you and pay you money? We do not pay you to tell us what we already know, but to make things worse than they are. We do not want reports; we want to see something real happen.'

'I'll do my best,' Mr Verloc started to say, but he stopped b   the other man was just looking hard at him.

'You're very fat,' the other man said rudely. He spoke in French.

'What did you say?' Mr Verloc asked.

Respectable people in London knew Mr Vladimir well, and liked him. He was amusing and told stories well. But Mr Verloc could see no amusement in his face. Mr Vladimir sat back in his chair and looked hard at Mr Verloc without moving his eyes.

'You understand French, don't you?' he said.

Mr Verloc explained that he was half French and lived there for a long time. He stood in the middle of the room holding his hat in one hand and feeling helpless. But then Mr Vladimir changed to English for the rest of the conversation.

'Ah, yes, of course,' he said. 'You were in prison there, weren't you? For five years? You sold us some secrets. How did they catch you?'

'A woman . . .' began Mr Verloc. 'She took my money, and told the police.'

'That wasn't very clever,' Mr Vladimir said. 'So what do you want?'

'I don't have anything to say,' said Mr Verloc. 'I got a letter. You wanted to see me.'

'How can you call yourself an anarchist?' Mr Vladimir said. 'You're too fat. You're not poor and hungry. I think you're lazy. And how long have we paid you from the Embassy here? How long have you worked for us in this country?'

'For eleven years,' said Mr Verloc. 'Since Baron Stott-Wartenheim was here. He used me several times. I came to London at first because he asked me to.'

'Ah, yes, the Baron,' said Mr Vladimir. 'Yes . . . he got a lot of soft, lazy people to work for us. But things must change. I asked you to come here to tell you this: you have to work for your money now. I see that you understand me. We don't want reports; we want action.'

'But only three months ago, when the Duke Romuald was

visiting Paris, I warned the Baron that some people wanted to try to kill the Duke. Don't you remember?'

'The French police didn't need your warning,' said Mr Vladimir. 'And now I repeat: we don't want words, we must have action. We want the British to wake up. Why do you anarchists just write stupid newspapers which nobody reads? You're all lazy. What can I do with you?'

'Why did you ask me to come here to the Embassy at eleven in the morning?' asked Mr Verloc, a little angry. He was better with words than with actions; he was unhappy that this young man was trying to get him to do something. 'It's dangerous for me to come here in the morning. If someone sees me, I'll stop being useful to you.'

'That's your problem,' said Mr Vladimir. 'When you stop being useful, we stop paying you.'

Mr Verloc's legs felt weak and he wanted suddenly to sit down.

'When I say that we want action,' Mr Vladimir went on, 'I don't mean that people have to die. We just want to frighten people. Buildings are enough. But which buildings? That's the question. What do you think, Mr Verloc?'

Mr Verloc didn't know. He said nothing. He was frightened of traps.

'I'll tell you,' Mr Vladimir said. 'Today people love and admire science. They thank science for their comfortable lives. So if we want to frighten them, we must attack a science building. The newspapers won't be able to use all their old, tired words to talk about *that*. Usually when a bomb attack happens, on a king, perhaps, or a theatre, people just say, "Oh, some poor people did that," and then they forget about it. But what about a bomb attack which people can't explain? *Then* they'll wake up. And it must be a famous building. I'll tell you the building that I'm thinking about, if you like. Can you guess?'

Mr Verloc just stood there, saying nothing. Mr Vladimir rested his arms on his desk, looked up at Mr Verloc and went on: 'The Greenwich Observatory!★ You see? Everyone in the world, rich and poor, has heard of the Greenwich Observatory. It's perfect!'

Mr Vladimir looked very pleased with himself. 'It won't be easy,' was all that Mr Verloc could say.

'What's the problem?' asked Mr Vladimir. 'You have a whole group of anarchists, don't you? Yundt is here in London – I've seen him. And there's Michaelis: he's out of prison now. Do you know where he is? If you don't, I can tell you. You mustn't think you're the only person that we pay.'

'It will cost money,' Mr Verloc said.

'Don't worry,' said Mr Vladimir. 'We'll still pay you every month – but first we must see some action. And if nothing happens soon, we'll stop paying you anything. What's your job – I mean, when you're not working for us?'

'I keep a shop,' answered Mr Verloc.

'A shop! What sort of shop?'

'Oh, newspapers and things. My wife . . .'

'Your wife? You're married? And you call yourself an anarchist!'

'Well, my wife isn't an anarchist. And it's none of your business.'

'Oh, yes, it is,' said Mr Vladimir. 'I'm not sure any more that you're the man for the job.' He was silent for a short time, thinking. Then he said, 'You can go now. You can have a month. There must be a bomb by then. Is that clear? If nothing happens, you'll stop working for us.'

He returned to the work on his desk, and Mr Verloc left the room. The same servant showed him out of the Embassy.

Mr Verloc walked back home without noticing anything. He went in and sat down at the back of the shop. No one came in to say anything to him. Stevie was cleaning the house upstairs. Mrs

★ The Greenwich Observatory is a famous building where scientists study the stars.

Verloc looked through the door when she heard the shop bell, but then returned to the kitchen when she saw that it was her husband.

An hour later she called towards the shop: 'Adolf!' Mr Verloc was still sitting in the same place. He got up heavily and came to dinner. People in this house didn't talk much, but Mr Verloc was strangely quiet at dinner. They could see that he was thinking hard. Winnie sat silent herself, watching Stevie. She did not want him suddenly to start talking. Every day she told him to be quiet and not to worry Mr Verloc.

When Stevie was very young, his mother and sister told him not to worry his father. After his father died, they told him not to worry the men who stayed at the hotel. And now they told him not to worry Mr Verloc. So Stevie admired Mr Verloc. He thought that Mr Verloc was an important man.

Mr Verloc did not notice Stevie much. Once Winnie's mother asked Winnie, 'Do you think that Mr Verloc is tired of having Stevie at your house?' And Winnie answered, 'He'll have to get tired of me first.'

'It was very sensible of you to marry Mr Verloc,' her mother said, but then stopped. She didn't understand. Why did Winnie marry an older man? There was that young man, the son of a butcher, but Winnie saw him only a few times. Then Mr Verloc started to stay at the hotel, and now ... Well, Winnie was very sensible.

Chapter 3   Talk, Talk, Talk

There was a meeting of the anarchist group in the back room behind Mr Verloc's shop. Michaelis was speaking. 'Things do not change because thinkers want them to change; things change because of the men with tools, because of the workers. What will happen next? You do not need to think about it. It's useless to think about it, because your thinking won't change anything. Do you understand?'

When Michaelis went into prison, he was thin. After fifteen years in prison, he came out fat. People said that a rich old woman was looking after Michaelis, by giving him money and sending him to doctors. She wanted to see him healthy again.

'You see,' he went on, 'prison gave me plenty of time to think about things.'

He was sitting on one side of the fire. In a chair on the other side – the chair in which Winnie usually sat – was Karl Yundt. He opened his mouth to laugh at Michaelis's words, and showed that there were no teeth in his mouth. He was old and had no hair on the top of his head, but a thin white beard below. He looked at the world with hard black eyes. Now he said, 'I always wanted to see a few men who were strong enough to kill others without pity. The world needs a group like this. That is the way for things to change for the better, if you ask me. But I could never find these men. There was only me.'

Mr Verloc, sitting on the sofa across the room, smiled his agreement.

'But you, Michaelis,' Yundt finished, 'you only want things to get worse.'

'That's not true!' said Michaelis. 'It's true that I see war between the rich and the poor, but in the end the workers will win and a new golden time will begin for man. In prison I *had* to think like this. It was either that or killing myself!'

The fourth person in the room, listening to this conversation, was Alexander Ossipon – they called him 'the Doctor'. For some years he was a student, because he wanted to be a doctor, but he left the university. Ossipon wrote most of the cheap newspapers which the anarchists tried to sell. Now he sat warming his feet in front of the fire. He had yellow hair and a strong, thick body. He wore a shirt and a tie under his coat, and his head rested on the back of the chair. From time to time he lifted a cigarette to his lips and blew smoke towards the ceiling.

Michaelis continued to talk. He talked to himself, really. Were the others listening? It didn't matter to him. He was better at talking to himself than at talking to others, because of his time in prison. And so he talked on and on ... but then a laugh from Ossipon cut his voice off. Michaelis looked surprised, and then he closed his eyes. The only sound in the room was the noise of the gas lights. With the fire and the lights, the room was starting to be very hot. Mr Verloc got up and opened the door into the kitchen. Now the men in the room could see Stevie, who was sitting at the kitchen table, making circles on pieces of paper. He did not turn or move his head to look at them; he just continued with his work.

Ossipon got up and went into the kitchen. He looked over Stevie's shoulder at the circles on the paper. When he came back to the others, he said, 'Of course, he's weak in the head. People like him are always making circles on paper, or something like that. The scientists' books are full of examples. If you read the books of Lombroso ...'

Mr Verloc's face went a little red. When he heard the word 'scientist' these days, he always thought of Mr Vladimir. He could almost see him in the room, standing in front of him with his clean-shaven face and his hard smile. But he said nothing.

'Lombroso is stupid,' said Karl Yundt.

'What do you mean?' asked Ossipon.

'Because when he wants to understand criminals, he looks in prisons. But the real criminals are not in prisons. The real criminals are the others, who put people in prisons. And it's stupid to think that you can look at people's teeth and ears and decide about them. If you want to know a prisoner ... well, the police burn numbers into prisoners' skin.'

Michaelis talked to himself, really. Were the others listening?
It didn't matter to him.

Michaelis smiled. Ossipon began to speak. 'You don't understand . . .' he said, but stopped, frightened by the look in Yundt's eyes.

Stevie got up from his chair just before Yundt began to speak. He wanted to go to bed, but when he was walking past the door, he heard Yundt talk of the police and burning. Stevie knew that hot metal on skin hurts. He stood still with his eyes wide open; his pieces of paper fell out of his hands and on to the floor. His mouth dropped open.

For a few minutes, after Yundt's angry words, no one spoke. Then Michaelis began again. He talked of the end of war, of the good times that were coming for all men.

'If you're right, Michaelis,' Ossipon said, 'we don't have to do anything. The good times will just come. But you're wrong. We can't be sure. There's only one important thing: the workers must feel angry. Then change will come, but it will not just come without action. This is science. Don't you agree, Verloc?'

But Verloc had nothing to say. He heard the word 'science' again and was quiet.

'Why are we thinking about tomorrow?' said Yundt. 'What about today? I think today the rich are eating the bodies of the poor and drinking their blood.'

At these frightening words, Stevie sat down hard on the floor. Before long the three anarchists left Mr Verloc and went home. Mr Verloc closed the door behind them with a crash. He was not pleased with his friends. He had a bomb to think about, and he could see that his friends were useless. They were lazy – Michaelis with his rich old woman, Ossipon with his girlfriends, Yundt with the woman who looked after him. And they did not know Vladimir. He was dangerous.

He turned off the gas lights and began to go to bed. Then he saw Stevie, who was in the kitchen, walking round the table and waving his hands. 'What's the boy doing there?' Mr Verloc asked himself. He didn't ask the boy because he spoke very little to him. In the morning, he said, 'Give me my boots,' and that was an order, not a question. So what could he say to the boy now? He had no idea.

He went upstairs and woke his wife. She went downstairs to look after Stevie, while Mr Verloc undressed and got ready for bed. When she came back into the room, he was sitting on the bed, looking at the floor.

'What are you doing there?' she asked.

'I don't feel very well,' he said. 'I have a headache.'

'Well, come to bed,' Winnie said. 'It's cold.'

He lay down in bed and looked up at the ceiling.

'Not many customers in the shop today,' said Winnie.

'No. Did you turn off the gas downstairs?'

'Yes, I did. That poor boy is very excited tonight. I think he heard some of your conversation. It's not good for him. He feels things very quickly and easily. If he hears bad things, he gets angry and excited.' She wanted her husband to know that Stevie was not bad, but just excited. She had to look after Stevie – and this meant that her husband must not think badly of the boy.

'He hears too much,' she went on. 'He was talking about burning skin and blood and things. He was saying, "Bad! Bad! Bad world for poor people!" It's not right. What were you talking about downstairs?'

'Ask Karl Yundt,' said Mr Verloc angrily.

'That man,' she said. 'I don't like him. Michaelis is all right.'

'I've had this headache for a few days now,' Mr Verloc said.

'Perhaps it was wrong to send Stevie to school,' Winnie said. 'He reads the newspapers from the shop, and gets angry at them too. There was a story the other day about a German soldier pulling off someone's ear. I couldn't do anything with Stevie that afternoon.'

Mr Verloc said nothing.

15

'Are you comfortable now, my dear?' she asked. 'Shall I turn off the light?'

Mr Verloc was sure that there was no sleep waiting for him that night. 'Yes,' he said. 'Turn off the light.'

Chapter 4   A Terrible Accident

Ossipon walked into the pub. There were about thirty tables against the walls. He bought himself a beer and looked for a place to sit. He saw a man at one of the tables, and looked surprised. He went over to the table and spoke to the man.

'You'll be able to help me to understand this business,' he said.

The little man with glasses waited for the noise in the pub to die down. Then he said, 'If I do know something, why do you think I'll tell you?' When he stopped talking he picked up the glass of beer from the table in front of him and had a long drink. Ossipon looked at the little man. He was small and weak, but he seemed so sure of himself. He spoke in short sentences, but was perfectly happy not to say anything sometimes.

Ossipon said, 'Have you been out much today?'

'No. I stayed in bed all the morning,' answered the other. 'Why?'

Ossipon *did* want to know something, but in front of this little man, the big Ossipon always felt small, so he said, 'Oh, nothing.' But then he tried another question: 'Did you walk down here?'

'No, I took a bus.' The little man lived in north London, in a room in a small house. His room was ordinary, but it had a very large cupboard. When the servant came to clean his room, the little man did not leave the room, but carefully watched the cleaner. When he left the house, he always locked his room and took his key with him.

16

'Have you been here long?' Ossipon asked.

'An hour or more,' answered the other.

'An hour,' said Ossipon. 'Then perhaps you haven't heard the news. I heard it only just now, in the street.'

The little man shook his head, but didn't seem to want to know the news. Ossipon said, 'I didn't know that you were in here. I just came in here for a drink.'

'Oh, I come here sometimes,' the other man said.

'It's strange that you, of all people, haven't heard the news,' Ossipon continued. 'You of all people.'

But still the little man said nothing. 'Do you give your explosives to anyone who asks you for them?' asked Ossipon.

'Yes, I never say no, as long as I have some to give,' answered the little man.

'Do you think you're right to do that?'

'Yes, I'm sure of it. Why not?'

'And if a detective asks you for some?'

'Hah! They don't come near me,' said the little man. 'They're too afraid. It's dangerous.'

'Why?'

'Because they know very well that I always have some explosives on me.' He touched the pocket of his coat lightly. 'It's in a thick bottle,' he said.

'Yes, people have told me,' Ossipon said. 'But if six of them jump on you and hold you, you won't be able to do anything.'

'You're wrong. I never walk outside after dark, and I always walk with my right hand in my pocket. I hold a rubber ball lightly in my hand. I only have to push this ball and twenty seconds later . . .'

'You have to wait twenty seconds!' said Ossipon. 'That's terrible!'

'It doesn't matter. I have the explosives, but that's not important. I'm brave enough to push the ball − that's the

'I have to tell you that a bomb killed a man in Greenwich Park
this morning.'

important thing. And the police know it, so they stay away from me. I'm the only true anarchist, you know. I never play. I work fourteen hours a day, and go hungry sometimes. Explosives cost money, so sometimes I don't have money for food. I see you're looking at my drink. Yes, I've had two beers already, and after this I'll have another one. Why not? I'm having a holiday.'

'I'm afraid you won't be happy after you've heard me,' said Ossipon. 'I have to tell you that a bomb killed a man in Greenwich Park this morning.'

'How do you know?'

'It's in the newspapers. I bought a paper and ran in here to read it. Then I saw you. I've got it in my pocket now.'

He pulled out the newspaper. 'Ah, here it is. Bomb in Greenwich Park, at half past eleven this morning. A foggy morning. Large hole in the ground under a tree. Pieces of a man's body all over the place, and leaves and bits of tree. They think the man was trying to bomb the Observatory.'

He gave the newspaper to the other man, who read it and put it down on the table. He didn't say anything.

'What have you done?' Ossipon asked. 'You didn't plan this, did you? Tell me, who did you give the explosives to?'

'All right, I'll tell you. Verloc.'

'Verloc! Impossible!'

'No, true, I'm afraid. He was an important man in your group, wasn't he?'

'More useful than important. And the police never seemed to notice him. That was good. He was married, you know. What will that woman do now?' He stopped to think.

The little man waited. He was called 'the Scientist' by his friends. No one knew his real name.

'Did Verloc tell you anything?' Ossipon asked at last. 'Why did he want the explosives?'

'He said they were for a building. The bomb was safe. "Put it against the building," I told him, "and then run away. In twenty minutes . . . boom!"'

'What went wrong, do you think?'

'I don't know. Perhaps he dropped it.'

'It's a bad time for this,' Ossipon said. 'Yundt is ill in bed: he's probably dying. Michaelis is out of town somewhere, writing a book. I'm the only one left now. I want the police to know that Verloc did this without us, without the help of the group. But how can I tell them?'

The Scientist was paying a waiter and getting ready to leave. Ossipon continued to think out loud. 'No, of course, the police don't know anything. Verloc is in small pieces. The police have no idea. Did anyone see him? Can anyone say, "It was Mr Verloc?" I don't think so. It was foggy. Good, good. Perhaps everything will be all right for the rest of us. Perhaps I'll go to the shop. I don't think that it's a trap.'

'Yes,' said the Scientist, the perfect anarchist, 'why don't you do that? Go to the woman.'

Chapter 5   A Bad Day for Heat

Detective Inspector Heat was having a bad day. First he missed breakfast. Then there was that bomb. He had to look at the bits of body. He felt sick. The body lay on a table in the Greenwich Park police station. While he was looking at the body, he asked the Park policeman, 'Did anyone see anything?'

'Yes, an old woman saw two men. They came out of the railway station and walked towards the park. One was a big man. The other was a young man with fair hair. And you can see that this man here' – he pointed to the bits on the table – 'had fair hair. The old woman said that he was carrying some kind of tin in his hand, and was walking a little behind the big man.'

'Do you know this old woman?'

'Yes, she's honest.'

'What about the big man?'

'She couldn't say. There was a lot of fog. She only really noticed the younger man.'

'What do you think happened?'

'I think that he fell over a stone in the park.'

'Yes,' said Detective Inspector Heat, 'that seems possible.' He saw on the table a piece of coat, and he picked it up. There was some writing on it. He took it over to the window for a better look. Now he could read the writing – and his face showed great surprise. He pushed the piece of coat into his pocket and left the police station.

He went back to London by train, thinking deeply. This piece of coat was very important. 'But what do I tell my boss, the Assistant Commissioner of Police?' he thought. 'Is it better to catch this bomber or not? I really don't know. Why did I find this piece of coat? It was so easy; it was like a present to me. But what do I do with this present, this information?'

Heat didn't like his work these days. He didn't like making reports to his bosses. It was an interesting problem. 'If I don't tell him all that I know,' he thought, 'he'll never know.'

He went to the Assistant Commissioner's office to make a report. The Assistant Commissioner was working at his desk. He looked up at Heat. 'What news from Greenwich?' he asked.

Detective Inspector Heat gave a clear report. He watched the sunlight on the Assistant Commissioner's desk and black hair. The Assistant Commissioner rested his head in his hands. When Heat finished, he waited. He was thinking, 'Do I tell him the rest?' But the Assistant Commissioner thought that he was waiting for him to speak.

'So you think that there were two men?' he said.

21

'Yes,' said Heat. 'The other man left the park unseen in the fog. He took the young man to the park and left him there to do the job. He was probably waiting back at the railway station when he heard the bomb. He knew it was too soon for the bomb, so he ran away.'

'Which train were the two men on?' said the Assistant Commissioner.

'I asked at the railway station. They came from Kent.★ The station guard remembers them. "The big man was carrying a shiny tin," he said, "and then he gave it to the young man." The young man followed the big man out of the station.'

'Who were these men?' the Assistant Commissioner went on. 'You told me this morning that they weren't from London. You didn't think that our London anarchists were bombers. So we have two foreign anarchists coming from Kent. That's very strange.'

'Perhaps it's not so strange, Assistant Commissioner. Michaelis is living near the station which they came from.'

Chapter 6   32 Brett Street

The important woman who looked after Michaelis and gave him money was a friend of the Assistant Commissioner's wife. Michaelis was in prison for a long time because he was an anarchist, not because he was a terrible criminal. When he was very young some people he knew wanted to save some men from prison. They asked Michaelis to help. He thought that it was an adventure, so he agreed to help. But the other men shot and killed one of the prison guards. The police caught Michaelis and threw him in prison. When he came out, the important woman

★ Part of south-east England, near London.

felt sorry for him. 'He's not dangerous,' she said, and the Assistant Commissioner agreed.

When Detective Inspector Heat spoke Michaelis's name, the Assistant Commissioner thought, 'What do I do now?' He didn't want to hurt the important woman, and he honestly didn't think that Michaelis was a dangerous bomber. The important woman was kind to him and to his wife – *that* was important to him, so he didn't want Michaelis to get into trouble. 'Prison will kill Michaelis; he won't come out alive.'

'Do you think Michaelis helped the bombers?' he asked Heat.

'Two bombers come from that part of Kent,' answered Heat. 'Yes, I think we must question Michaelis.'

The Assistant Commissioner was worried. When he was younger, he was an adventurous policeman and detective. Now he was sitting behind a desk, and men like Heat could change everything for him, while he could do nothing. But perhaps he could. A plan was beginning to come to him.

'If Michaelis is so important,' he said, 'why didn't you speak of him immediately? You gave your report. You were in my office for twenty minutes before speaking his name. I think that you were thinking of another person at first. If I'm right, tell me: who is this other person?'

Detective Inspector Heat was surprised. The Assistant Commissioner was very clever. 'If I don't tell him about that piece of coat now,' he thought, 'I'll be in big trouble.'

'Yes,' he said, 'I was coming to that part of my report.'

'What have you got?' asked the Assistant Commissioner.

'I have an address,' answered the Detective Inspector, pulling the piece of coat out of his pocket. 'This belongs to the bomber: he was wearing it when he died. Look at this.'

The Assistant Commissioner took the burned piece of coat. He could see on it a number and two words: 32 Brett Street. He was surprised.

'Why did the bomber have his address on his coat?' he asked. 'Parents do that for their children sometimes, but this man was no child. But what is 32 Brett Street, Detective Inspector. Do you know?'

'It's a shop,' said the Detective Inspector.

The Assistant Commissioner waited, but Heat said nothing more. The Assistant Commissioner had to question him. At last he heard Mr Verloc's name. He looked up at the Detective Inspector.

'And you say that we don't have this man's name on paper here in this office?'

'That's right. It was enough for me to know him, and to use him when I wanted to. A friend of mine in the French police told me he was an Embassy spy. When Baron Stott-Wartenheim was at the Embassy, this man Verloc gave us some very useful information. Later, I met him again. I told him that I knew he was a secret agent. He said he didn't want any trouble; he just wanted to look after his shop. "If you don't do anything wrong," I said, "you needn't worry about trouble from the police. Shops like yours are not usually safe from us, but yours will be. But if I help you, you must help me too." And so from time to time, when I want some information, he gives it to me.'

'But he didn't give you any information this time,' said the Assistant Commissioner.

'I didn't ask him anything, so he didn't tell me anything,' explained the Detective Inspector. 'My guess is that he knows nothing about this bomb.'

'Then how do you explain this?' asked the Assistant Commissioner, pointing to the burned piece of coat.

'I don't know. I don't understand it. I think that Michaelis will be able to tell us more about the bomb than Verloc.'

'You do? What about the other man, who escaped from the park in the fog?'

'He must be far away by now,' said Heat.

'I don't know. I don't understand it. I think that Michaelis will be able to tell us more about the bomb than Verloc.'

The Assistant Commissioner thought for a short time. He didn't want to sit behind his desk; he wanted action. He sent the Detective Inspector away, and then he picked up his hat and left the office. He found a carriage and told the driver to take him to Brett Street.

Chapter 7   Sad News for Winnie

A few weeks before the Assistant Commissioner decided on his plan, Mr Verloc went to Europe to buy things for his shop. He was away for ten days. When he came back, he seemed tired. He walked into the shop and sat down immediately in a chair. Stevie was cleaning the shop. He stopped and looked at Mr Verloc in admiration.

'Here!' said Mr Verloc, and kicked his suitcase. Stevie ran over and took the suitcase upstairs.

Winnie heard the shop bell and she came in. 'You'll want some breakfast,' she said.

While he ate breakfast, Winnie talked to him about the shop. 'We had quite a few customers while you were away,' she said. 'Oh, yes, and I saw Michaelis two or three times. He told me that he's going to stay in Kent for a few weeks. He's going to write a book. And Karl Yundt visited once – terrible man.' She did not speak of Ossipon, but her face turned a little red. 'Stevie was unhappy while you were away. I don't mean that he wasn't useful round the house: he's always helpful. But he likes to see you and be near you. He admires you a lot. You only have to ask him, and he'll do anything for you.'

After breakfast Mr Verloc said, 'I'm going out for a walk.'

'Why don't you take Stevie with you?' asked Winnie.

Mr Verloc was surprised. It was a new idea. 'But if he loses me, can he find his way home?' he said.

'He won't lose you; he wants to be near you,' said Winnie. 'But I'm sure that someone will bring him back. You needn't worry.'

This was Mr Verloc's second surprise. Why was she so sure?

'All right. He can come with me.'

At the shop door, Winnie watched them. The two of them walked down the street, one tall and fat, the other short and thin. 'They look like a father and son,' she thought proudly.

Over the next few days, she was pleased to see that Mr Verloc seemed to like going out for walks with Stevie. Now, when he was ready to go out, he called to Stevie: 'Let's go!' They went out together every day. And in the house Mr Verloc watched Stevie. But Stevie sat in corners and talked to himself. She couldn't quite hear him. 'What are you saying, Stevie?' she asked, but he just looked angry and didn't say anything. She was worried. 'What do you tell him during your walks together?' she asked Mr Verloc.

'Oh, nothing, really,' said Mr Verloc. 'You wanted Stevie to come out for walks with me. Remember?'

The next day Mr Verloc said, 'I think Stevie needs a change. I'm going to take him to stay with Michaelis in Kent. Stevie will enjoy the fresh green trees and the animals.'

That day Stevie was more angry than usual. Winnie could hear some of the things he was saying: 'Bad world for poor people! Poor people must eat. If they're poor, perhaps they steal from rich people. Police hurt them, put them in prison.' On and on he went, sitting in his corner. She was worried, but she was pleased at Mr Verloc's kindness. It was good of him to take Stevie to stay with Michaelis.

On the day of the bomb in Greenwich Park, Mr Verloc went out very early in the morning and did not come back until nearly dark. She was sitting in the shop when Mr Verloc came in with the sound of the bell. She didn't look up from her work.

'The weather's bad, isn't it? Did you see Stevie today?'

'No, I didn't,' said Mr Verloc softly.

Some time later Winnie got up to go into the kitchen. 'Soon he'll want his supper,' she thought. But when she went into the back room, she saw that Mr Verloc was sitting by the fire.

'I think I've caught a cold,' he said.

'Did you get wet?' she asked. 'Where were you today?'

'Nowhere,' he said, but then a little later: 'I went to the bank. I took out the money.'

'What do you mean? All of it?'

'Yes.'

'Why?'

He didn't reply at first. She put some bread and cold meat on the table.

'Why don't you take off your shoes?' she said. 'They're all wet. You're not going out again tonight.'

Then he started to speak. 'Well,' he said, 'you see . . . I thought . . . I . . . if I suddenly have to go to France . . . I mean, go to live there . . . or California, perhaps.'

'That's a strange idea,' she said. 'Why will you have to go? The shop is doing all right. We're comfortable here.' She looked round the room. This was Stevie's home too. What about him?

Mr Verloc said nothing. Winnie came and gave him a kiss, but he sat in his chair without moving. She cleaned the table. His eyes followed her movements.

'If you go and live in France or somewhere,' she said, 'you'll have to go without me.' She was thinking of Stevie. He must stay here, in this country. 'But you won't go. You need me too much.'

Just then they heard the sound of the shop bell. 'Shop, Adolf,' she said. 'You go.'

Mr Verloc went into the shop. Winnie washed some cups and plates. He was a long time in the shop. 'It must be a customer,' she thought. She listened, but she couldn't hear voices.

'If you go and live in France or somewhere,' she said, 'you'll have to go
without me.' She was thinking of Stevie.

When Mr Verloc came back, his face was white. 'I have to go out,' he said. Winnie went into the shop and looked at the man who was waiting there. He was tall and well dressed. He didn't look like a customer.

She returned to the back room. Mr Verloc was putting on his coat. 'Who is that man?' she asked. 'Do you know him?'

'I've heard of him,' he said uneasily.

'He's not from the Embassy, is he?'

'Embassy!' Mr Verloc said in surprise. 'What Embassy? Who has said anything to you about Embassies?'

'You have, my dear,' she said. 'You were talking in your sleep.'

'What did I say?' Mr Verloc seemed frightened.

'Nothing sensible. But I knew that you were worried.'

'Those Embassy people!' said Mr Verloc. 'I want to cut their hearts out.' He pushed his hat on his head and started to go out.

'Adolf!' she called after him. 'What about the money? Give me the money.'

'Oh, yes,' he said. He gave her the money and she hid it among her clothes immediately, without looking at it. Then he went away with the visitor.

Winnie felt afraid. What was happening? Everything was mysterious and worrying. She felt danger all round her. Suddenly she heard the sound of the shop bell again. She went into the shop. A man was standing there.

'Is your husband at home, Mrs Verloc?' the man asked.

'No, he's gone out.'

'I'm sorry about that. I came to give him some information.'

This was true. When Detective Inspector Heat left the office, he went home, but then he decided to go to Brett Street. He wanted to warn Mr Verloc.

'When will your husband be back?' he asked. 'Do you know?'

'No,' she said.

'I'm Detective Inspector Heat of the police,' he said. 'Why did your husband go out? I want you to tell me.'

'I don't know,' she said. 'He went out with another man, a stranger.'

'Tell me about this stranger. What did he look like?'

Winnie told him. Heat's face turned darker. 'The Assistant Commissioner was quick,' he thought. To Winnie he said, 'I haven't got the time to wait for your husband now.'

Winnie said nothing. 'What do you know about this business?' Heat asked.

'What business? Nothing. I've stayed at home all day.'

'So you haven't seen any newspapers?'

'No.'

'Have you lost a coat – a coat with your address in it?' He showed her the piece of coat.

'That's my brother's coat. What do you mean?'

'Can I see your brother? Where is he?'

'He's not here. He's out of town, staying with a friend.'

'What's the name of this friend?'

'His name's Michaelis.'

Heat's eyes flew open in surprise.

'Interesting,' he said. 'And your brother – is he a big man with dark hair like yours?'

'No, he's short, with fair hair. But where did he lose his coat?'

Heat felt in his pocket for the piece of coat. He pulled it out and showed it to her. 'This is from my brother's coat,' she said. 'Who burned it like this?'

Heat sat down heavily in a chair. Now he knew that Verloc was the other man at the park.

'Mrs Verloc,' he said, 'I think you know more about this bomb than you think.'

They heard the sound of the bell. Mr Verloc walked into the shop. 'What are you doing here?' he asked the detective.

'I must talk to you,' Heat said. 'Come in here.'

They went into the back room. Winnie listened at the door. She could not hear everything that they said.

'You were the other man in the park, Verloc,' said Heat, and then a little later: 'Look! It has your address on it!'

'I didn't know,' said Mr Verloc.

'You must get away now,' Heat said. 'Go to Europe or somewhere. But how did you escape from the park?'

'I heard the bomb. It was too soon. I was waiting for him. I just ran away.'

'We think he fell,' the Detective Inspector said a little later. 'There were only bits of his body. You must go away.'

'Where will I go?' said Verloc. 'I told that other man, the Assistant Commissioner, that I wanted to stay and give a full report to the police. And I really do want to do that. I'm tired. I want to stay here with my wife, in this country, looking after my shop.'

Soon after that the Inspector left. Mrs Verloc sat in the shop, with her mouth open. She didn't cry; she didn't say a word. In her head she heard the words: 'Only bits of his body . . . only bits of his body.'

Chapter 8   Murder!

'She knows all about it now,' Mr Verloc thought. He looked at his wife. She was still sitting in the shop. 'She said to me, "You needn't worry." She said, "I'm sure that someone will bring Stevie home." Now I understand. She put the address in his coat. Why didn't she tell me?'

Mr Verloc went into the shop. 'I didn't mean to hurt the boy,' he said. 'It's all because of that terrible man at the Embassy.'

Mrs Verloc shut her eyes. She hid her face in her hands.

'Now, Winnie,' said Mr Verloc, 'we have to think of tomorrow. The police will come and get me. What will you do then?'

Mrs Verloc didn't move.

'Why don't you look at me?'

'I don't want to look at you as long as I live.'

'What? You don't mean that. Now, come out of the shop. You can't sit here.' There was no answer. He decided to try to be kind, instead of giving orders. 'This won't bring him back, you know,' he said.

Was she hearing him? He didn't know. He waited for a long time, but nothing happened. 'Don't be stupid, Winnie,' he said.

It was impossible to talk to a woman who was hiding her face in her hands. He held her hands and tried to pull them away from her face, but she kept her hands there and he pulled her off the chair. She ran into the back room.

After a time Mr Verloc followed her. First he turned off the gas lights in the shop and locked the door. He felt very tired. His work as a secret agent was at an end; he was on his way to prison.

'Why don't you go to bed?' he said. 'You need a good cry.'

While Mr Verloc went on and on, Mrs Verloc stood silently. Why was he talking? What was he talking about? Then a picture came into her head. Mr Verloc and Stevie were walking down the street together. 'They looked like a father and son,' she said.

'What? What did you say?' said Mr Verloc, but then he went on talking about someone at some Embassy. Winnie looked at the wall. She tried to remember something. What was it? Something terrible was happening. Then she remembered: 'This man took the boy away to murder him. He took the boy from his home to murder him. He took the boy away from me to murder him!' She hated him.

He didn't understand. She loved the boy with all her heart. She had to look after him. The butcher's son wanted to marry her, and she liked him, but he was poor: he couldn't pay for

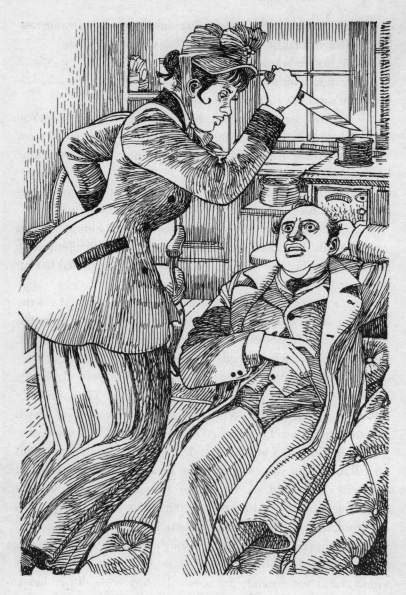

When she came to the sofa Mr Verloc opened his eyes.
She brought the knife down just once ...

Stevie. So she found Mr Verloc. She did everything for Stevie, and now Stevie was dead because of this man.

'You didn't know,' the man was saying. 'You brought the police here, with that address. But it's all right. I won't leave you. I like you too much.'

Mrs Verloc wanted to get away. She went upstairs. 'That's right,' he called out. 'You go and sleep'. But when she was upstairs, she only opened the window. It was not very far from the ground. She wanted to kill herself, but it was not high enough.

Mr Verloc felt very hungry. He cut some meat with a knife and ate it with some bread. He lay down on the sofa to rest. He could hear his wife upstairs. She was changing her clothes, he thought. When she came back downstairs, she was wearing her coat. Now she felt free.

'Where are you going?' Mr Verloc asked. 'It's too late to go out. You must stay here with me this evening. Why don't you talk to me? Say *something*, won't you?'

Mrs Verloc understood that she was not free. As long as this man was alive, she was not free.

'Winnie,' he said.

'Yes.'

'Come here.'

She walked over to the sofa. There was a knife on the table. She picked it up. When she came to the sofa Mr Verloc opened his eyes. She brought the knife down just once deep into his body and left it there. Mr Verloc died immediately.

She sat down. Now she was free. She didn't move, she didn't think. She was quiet, and the body of Mr Verloc on the sofa was quiet. He died without making a noise: no sound broke the respectability of their home. Everything was quiet and respectable.

She sat there for a long time, with her eyes on the ground. But then she looked up. There was a noise somewhere. What was it? She saw a black pool of something on the floor under the sofa. It was blood. Blood was dropping from Mr Verloc's side on to the floor.

Chapter 9   The Great Escape

Mrs Verloc quickly got up from the chair and ran out of the room. She unlocked the shop door and ran out into the street. She must be calm. She didn't want to die. 'I murdered my husband. They'll kill me,' she thought. 'I must escape. I must go to Europe.'

Out on the street she ran into the arms of a man. The man held her and looked at her. 'Mrs Verloc!' he said.

'Mr Ossipon,' she answered. 'What are you doing here?'

'I was coming to help you,' he said. 'Where were you going?' He still held her arm. Ossipon was not afraid of women. He had a lot of women friends. He was interested in women, and it was his luck always to find women. So he was not surprised to find Mrs Verloc in his arms.

'Perhaps I was going to find you, Tom,' she said.

Ossipon was excited that she called him 'Tom'. It was a personal name, used only by his best friends. 'I'm ready to help you,' he said.

'What do you know about my trouble?' she asked. He worried her.

'I read about the bomb in the newspaper. I met a man who gave me information. I knew that Mr Verloc was dead. Then I came over here. You know that I love you, don't you?'

'Yes, I know, Tom.'

'You've seen it in my eyes. But you never told me that you knew.'

'Of course not. I was a respectable woman.'

'I always thought that he was the wrong husband for you. But you seemed to live happily with him. You seemed to love him.'

'Love him!' she said. 'No, I didn't love him. I wanted my brother to be as comfortable as possible. I never loved my husband.'

'But he's dead now.'

She put her hand on his arm. 'You know that he's dead?'

Ossipon didn't understand. What was this woman talking about? Of course he knew that Verloc was dead.

'How did you first hear about it?' he asked.

'From the police.'

'The police were here already?'

'Yes. They showed me a piece of coat. And there was another man too. Perhaps he was from the Embassy . . .'

'Embassy? What Embassy?'

'I don't know. Don't ask me questions, please, Tom. I'm tired.'

'All right,' Ossipon said. 'I won't.'

'You must hide me somewhere until the morning,' she said. 'Then we can go to Europe together.'

'But I have no money,' said Ossipon.

'Don't worry. I have plenty of money,' she said. 'He gave it to me.'

Ossipon thought, 'Who gave it to her?' But he didn't ask her. He said, 'I think we're all right. There's a boat at midnight and a train from Waterloo station at 10.30. We can catch that train, and by the morning we'll be in France!'

'I think that I left the light on in the house,' she said. 'Will you turn it off for me?'

'Is the money in the house?' he asked.

'No, I've got it on me. Please . . . just go and turn off the light in the back room. I don't want anyone to see it.'

She pushed him inside and he walked through the shop into

the back room. First he saw Mr Verloc's hat in the middle of the floor. Then he saw the dark pool of blood. His eyes moved towards the sofa . . . He turned back into the shop and was sick. Was this a trap? What was happening? He ran towards the shop door, but just then Mrs Verloc came inside.

'There's a policeman on the street,' she said quietly. 'I think he saw me. If he comes in, you must kill me. You will, won't you?'

But the policeman walked on past the house. After a few minutes Ossipon and Mrs Verloc left the shop. They found a carriage which took them to Waterloo. 'They mustn't catch me,' Winnie said, 'I don't want to die. I'll stay with you for ever. I . . . I won't ask you to marry me.'

'Was he asleep?' Ossipon asked.

'No, he was talking. He took the boy away to kill him. He killed the boy and then he lay quite easy on the sofa. "Come here," he told me. Do you hear, Tom? he said, "Come here," after taking my heart along with my poor boy. Help me!' she cried. 'You must help me!'

'When we arrive at the station,' he said, 'you must get on to the train before me. I'll meet you there. Nobody must see us together. Clear?'

'Yes.'

'Give me the money now. I'll buy the tickets. Here we are now, at the station. Go on. Get on the train. I'll come in a minute.'

'There's no danger, is there, Tom? I'll be safe?'

'Yes, perfectly safe, my dear. Don't worry about a thing.'

He bought the tickets and found her on the train. 'Oh, Tom,' she said. 'How can I thank you? I was afraid, but you've helped me. I'm not afraid now. I'll live for you always, Tom.'

When the train started to move, Ossipon got up. He opened the door and jumped out on to the platform. He fell down and people came over to him. 'Are you all right?' they asked. He picked himself up and laughed. 'Yes,' he said. 'There's no problem. My sister was crying, and I stayed too long on the train to look after her. But I'm not hurt. Do you see? I can walk.' And he left the station, laughing quietly to himself.

◆

A few days later he was drinking beer with the Scientist in the same pub. In his pocket was a newspaper. Some words from the newspaper were running through his head. 'A mystery,' the newspaper said. 'Why did the young woman throw herself off the ship to France? Why did she kill herself? What trouble was she in?' Ossipon hated himself.

ACTIVITIES

Chapters 1–3

Before you read

1 What is a secret agent? Use your dictionary to find out. What sort
   of work do they do? Can you think of a very short word in English
   which means the same as 'secret agent'?

2 Find these words in your dictionary.
   action   admire   carriage
   Which word means:
   a something with four wheels which is pulled by horses
   b to think a person is good or important
   c something that you do

3 Find these words in your dictionary.
   anarchist   bomb   revolution
   The story in this book happens in England in the 1880s. There were
   quite a lot of *anarchists* in Europe in those days. What do you know
   about anarchists? Tell another student. Then write two sentences
   about anarchists with the following words: *revolution, bomb.*

4 Find these words in your dictionary.
   bell   Embassy   respectable   trap
   Now use the words to finish these sentences.
   a An . . . . . is the office of a foreign country in your country.
   b A . . . . . is something which catches people or animals.
   c A . . . . . makes a musical sound.
   d A . . . . . person is someone who seems to do the right things.

After you read

5 Who are these people? Put the names on the left with the words
   on the right.
   a Mr Verloc   works in a foreign Embassy.
   b Mr Ossipon   is Mr Verloc's pretty young wife.
   c Mr Vladimir   owns a small shop.
   d Stevie   is one of Mr Verloc's friends.
   e Winnie   is Winnie's problem brother.

6 At the anarchists' meeting, Michaelis says, 'In the end the workers

will win and a new golden time will begin for man.' Do you agree with this? Why/why not?

Chapters 4–6

Before you read

7   What do you think Mr Verloc is going to do? Do you think he *can* put a bomb in the Greenwich Observatory? Why/why not?

8   Find these words in your dictionary.
    explosive   foggy
    a   What sort of people use *explosives*? Why? When? Where?
    b   What is the weather like in your country? Is it ever *foggy*? What sort of accidents can happen when it is foggy?

After you read

9   Answer these questions:
    a   What is strange about the Scientist's room?
    b   What news does Ossipon tell the Scientist?
    c   What is Stevie carrying when he goes into the park?
    d   Where is Michaelis living when he is writing his book?
    e   Who does the Detective Inspector want to save? Why?
    f   What is the address of Mr Verloc's shop? Why is this address on Stevie's coat?

10 People still use bombs today to frighten and kill others. Think of reasons why people do this.

Chapters 7–9

Before you read

11 Look at the picture on page 34. What is the woman with the knife going to do? Why?

After you read

12 Who says these words? Who to?
    a   'Those Embassy people! I want to cut their hearts out.'
    b   'There were only bits of his body. You must go away.'
    c   'I don't want to look at you as long as I live.'
    d   'If he comes in, you must kill me.'

41

13 Work with another student. Have a conversation.

Student A: You are Mr Verloc. You are out walking with Stevie.
             Tell him what you want to change in the world.

Student B: You are Stevie. Ask Mr Verloc questions about what
             anarchists think and do.

Writing

14 Tell the story again through Winnie's eyes. How does she live?
Does her husband seem strange to her? What are her feelings for
Stevie? What does she feel after she hears about the bomb?

15 You are the policeman who finds the dead body in the park after
the bomb. Write a report. What do you do? What do you see? Who
do you talk to?

16 No one in *The Secret Agent* is happy or good. Even the policemen
are just trying to help their friends. Do you think that Conrad gives
us a picture of the real world? Why/why not?

17 Did you find the story exciting? Did you always want to ask, 'What
will happen next? Who has died in the park? How does Conrad
keep the story exciting?

Answers for the Activities in this book are published in our free resource packs for teachers, the
Penguin Readers Factsheets, or available on a separate sheet. Please write to your local Pearson
Education office or to: Marketing Department, Penguin Longman Publishing, 80 Strand,
London WC2R 0RL